Cool LUNCHES to make & take

Easy Recipes for Kids to Cook

Lisa Wagner

ABDO
Publishing Company

TO ADULT HELPERS

You're invited to assist an up-and-coming chef in a kitchen near you! And it will pay off in many ways. Your children can develop new skills, gain confidence, and make some delicious food while learning to cook. What's more, it's going to be a lot of fun!

These recipes are designed to let children cook independently as much as possible. Encourage them to do whatever they are able to do on their own. Also encourage them to try the variations supplied with each recipe and to experiment with their own ideas. Building creativity into the cooking process encourages children to think like real chefs.

Before getting started, set some ground rules about using the kitchen, cooking tools, and ingredients. Most important, adult supervision is a must whenever a child uses the stove, oven, or sharp tools. (Look for the Hot Stuff! and Super Sharp! symbols.)

So, put on your aprons and stand by. Let your young chefs take the lead. Watch and learn. Taste their creations. Praise their efforts. Enjoy the culinary adventure!

Visit us at www.abdopublishing.com

Published by ABDO Publishing Company, 4940 Viking Drive, Edina, Minnesota 55435. Copyright © 2007 by Abdo Consulting Group, Inc. International copyrights reserved in all countries. No part of this book may be reproduced in any form without written permission from the publisher. The Checkerboard Library™ is a trademark and logo of ABDO Publishing Company.

Printed in the United States.

Design and Production: Mighty Media, Inc.
Art Direction: Anders Hanson
Photo Credits: Anders Hanson, Shutterstock
Series Editor: Pam Price

The following manufacturers/names appearing in this book are trademarks: Pyrex®, Reynolds® Cut-Rite® Waxed Paper, Target® Aluminum Foil, Target® Plastic Wrap, Freez Pak® Reusable Ice Substitute, Hellmann's® Mayonnaise, M&M's®, Lunds® and Byerlys® Chianti Red Wine Vinegar, Morton® Iodized Salt, Blue Ice® Reusable Ice Substitute, Minute Maid® Apple Strawberry Juice

Library of Congress Cataloging-in-Publication Data

Wagner, Lisa, 1958-
  Cool lunches to make & take : easy recipes for kids to cook / Lisa Wagner.
      p. cm. -- (Cool cooking)
  Includes index.
  ISBN-13: 978-1-59928-723-2
  ISBN-10: 1-59928-723-4
  1. Lunchbox cookery--Juvenile literature. I. Title. II. Title: Cool lunches to make and take.

  TX735.W32 2007
  641.5'3--dc22
                              2006032081

Table of Contents

WHAT MAKES COOKING SO COOL 4

THE BASICS 5

THE TOOL BOX 8

COOL COOKING TERMS 10

THE COOLEST INGREDIENTS 12

SUPER-DUPER SUBS 16

SALAD IN YOUR POCKET 18

MAKE IT A WRAP! 21

MAKE IT & TAKE IT 22

CREATE-A-KABOB 24

HIT THE TRAIL MIX 27

PASTA SALAD PRESTO 28

GLOSSARY 31

WEB SITES 31

INDEX 32

What Makes Cooking So Cool

Welcome to the world of cooking! The cool thing about cooking is that you are the chef! You get to decide what to cook, how to cook, and what ingredients you want to use.

Everything you need to know to get started is in this book. You will learn the basic cooking terms and tools. All of the recipes in this book require only basic kitchen equipment. All the tools you will need are pictured on pages 8 through 9.

Most of the ingredients used in these recipes are shown on pages 12 through 15. This will help you identify the items for your grocery list. You want to find the freshest ingredients possible when shopping. You may notice some foods marked *organic*. This means that the food was grown using earth-friendly fertilizers and pest control methods.

The fun part of this book is that all of the recipes are for foods you can make and take. Make your own special lunch and take it to school. Make a picnic and take your friends to the park. Make a tasty snack and take it to a party.

Most of the recipes have variations, so you can be creative. A recipe can be different every time you make it. Get inspired and give a recipe your original touch. Being a cook is like being an artist in the kitchen. The most important ingredient is imagination!

GET THE PICTURE!

When a step number in a recipe has a dotted circle around it, look for the picture that goes with it. The circle around the photo will be the same color as the step number.

4 →

The Basics

Get going in the right direction
with a few important basics!

ASK PERMISSION

> Before you cook, get permission to use the kitchen, cooking tools, and ingredients.

> If you'd like to do everything by yourself, say so. As long as you can do it safely, do it.

> When you need help, ask. Always get help when you use the stove or oven.

BE PREPARED

> Being well organized is a chef's secret ingredient for success!

> Read through the entire recipe before you do anything else.

> Gather all your cooking tools and ingredients.

> Get the ingredients ready. The list of ingredients tells how to prepare each item.

> Put each prepared ingredient into a separate bowl.

> Read the recipe instructions carefully. Do the steps in the order they are listed.

BE SMART, BE SAFE

> If you use the stove or oven, you need an adult in the kitchen with you.

> Never use the stove or oven if you are home alone!

> Always get an adult to help with the hot jobs, such as draining boiling water.

> Have an adult nearby when you are using a sharp tool such as a knife, peeler, or grater. Always use sharp tools with care.

> Always turn pot handles toward the back of the stove. This helps prevent you from accidentally knocking over pots.

> Prevent accidents by working slowly and carefully. Take your time.

> If you get hurt, let an adult know right away!

BE NEAT AND CLEAN

> Start with clean hands, clean tools, and a clean work surface.

> Tie back long hair so it stays out of the way and out of the food.

> Wear comfortable clothing and roll up your sleeves.

> Aprons and chef hats are optional!

No Germs Allowed!

After you handle raw eggs or raw meat, wash your hands with soap and water. Wash tools and work surfaces with soap and water too. Raw eggs and raw meat have bacteria that can't survive being cooked. But the bacteria can survive at room or body temperature. These bacteria can make you very sick if you consume them. So, keep everything clean!

KEY SYMBOLS

In this book, you will see some symbols beside the recipes. Here is what they mean.

HOT STUFF!

The recipe requires the use of a stove or oven. You need adult assistance and supervision.

SUPER SHARP!

A sharp tool such as a peeler, knife, or grater is needed. Get an adult to stand by.

EVEN COOLER!

This symbol means adventure! It could be a tip for making the recipe spicier. Sometimes it's a wild variation using an unusual ingredient. Give it a try! Get inspired and invent your own super-cool ideas.

MEASURING

Most ingredients are measured by the cup, tablespoon, or teaspoon.

Measuring cups and spoons come in a variety of sizes. An amount is printed or **etched** on each one to show how much it holds. To measure ½ cup, use the measuring cup marked ½ cup and fill it to the top.

Ingredients such as meat and cheese are measured by weight in ounces or pounds. You purchase them by weight too.

TIP: Set a measuring cup inside a large bowl to catch spills. Hold a measuring spoon over a small bowl or cup to catch spills.

The Tool Box

A box on the bottom of the first page of each recipe lists the tools you need. When you come across a tool you don't know, turn back to these pages.

SERRATED KNIFE

SMALL SHARP KNIFE

CUTTING BOARD

MEASURING CUPS

MEASURING SPOONS

GLASS MEASURING CUP

PREP BOWLS

WOODEN SPOON

MELON SCOOP

MIXING BOWLS

SPOON

RUBBER SPATULA

PEELER

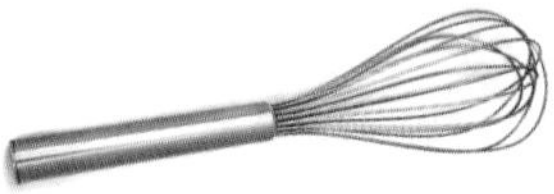

WHISK

CAN OPENER

FORK

BAKING SHEET

STRAINER OR COLANDER

SAUCEPAN

SKEWERS

WAXED PAPER

4-QUART POT

TOOTHPICKS

PLASTIC WRAP

SOFT-SIDED LUNCH BOX

PLASTIC CONTAINER

REUSABLE ICE BLOCKS

RESEALABLE BAGS

TOWELS

TIMER

POT HOLDER

PEPPER GRINDER

SMALL COOLER

9

Cool Cooking Terms

You need to learn the basic cooking terms and the actions that go with them. Whenever you need to remind yourself, just turn back to these pages.

Most ingredients need preparation before they are cooked or assembled. Look at the list of ingredients beside the recipe. After some items, you'll see words such as *chopped*, *sliced*, or *diced*. These words tell you how to prepare the ingredients.

FIRST THINGS FIRST

Always wash fruit and vegetables well. Rinse them under cold water. Pat them dry with a towel. Then they won't slip when you cut them.

PEEL

Peel means to remove the skin. Use a peeler for carrots, potatoes, cucumbers, and apples. Hold the item to be peeled against the cutting board. Slide the peeler away from you along the surface of the food.

TIP: To peel onion or garlic, remove the papery shell. Trim each end with a sharp knife. Then peel off the outer layer with your fingers. Never put garlic or onion peels in a food disposer!

CHOP

Chop means to cut things into small pieces. The more you chop, the smaller the pieces. If a recipe says finely chopped, it means you need very small pieces.

TIP: When you slice or chop round foods, such as carrots, get a grip! Cut a lengthwise slice off one side. Put the flat side on the cutting board. Now the food won't roll when you cut it.

CUBE OR DICE

Cube and *dice* mean to cut cube or dice shapes. Usually *dice* refers to smaller pieces, and *cube* refers to larger pieces. Often a recipe will give you a dimension, such as ¼-inch dice.

TIP: Use two steps to dice or cube. First make all your cuts going one direction. Then turn the cutting board and make the crosscuts.

SLICE

Slice means to cut food into pieces of the same thickness.

WHISK

Whisk means to beat quickly by hand. The tool you use to whisk is also called a whisk. Move the whisk using a circular motion. If you don't have a whisk, you can use a fork instead.

GRATE

Grate means to shred something into small pieces using a grater. A grater has surfaces covered in holes with raised, sharp edges. You rub the food against a surface using firm pressure.

MIX

When you mix, you stir ingredients together, usually with a large spoon. *Blend* is another word for *mix*.

The Coolest Ingredients

FRENCH BREAD

EGGS

POCKET BREAD

TORTILLAS

BOW TIE PASTA

MAYONNAISE

HAM

ROAST BEEF

CANNED TUNA

SALAMI

ROAST TURKEY

PARMESAN CHEESE

PROVOLONE CHEESE

MOZZARELLA CHEESE

SWISS CHEESE

CHEDDAR CHEESE

GREEN PEPPER

CELERY

LEAF LETTUCE

CUCUMBER

RED ONION

GARLIC

CARROTS

CHERRY TOMATOES

SCALLIONS

RADISHES

TOMATO

GRAPES

STRAWBERRIES

CANTALOUPE

Allergy Alert

Some people have a reaction when they eat certain kinds of food. If you have any allergies, you know what it's all about. An allergic reaction can require emergency medical help. Nut allergies are serious and can be especially **dangerous**. Before you serve anything made with nuts, ask if anyone has a nut allergy. People with nut allergies will not be able to eat what you have prepared. Don't be offended. It might save a life!

SUNFLOWER SEEDS

CASHEWS

PEANUTS

YOGURT-DIPPED RAISINS

PRETZEL CHUNKS

CHOCOLATE CHIPS

ALMONDS

RAISINS

DRIED CRANBERRIES

DRIED CHERRIES

COATED CHOCOLATE CANDIES

OLIVE OIL

RED WINE VINEGAR

SALT

SESAME STICKS

PEPPERCORNS

DRIED OREGANO

DRIED BASIL

GROUND BLACK PEPPER

FRESH BASIL

FRESH PARSLEY

FRESH OREGANO

Peppercorns

Ground pepper comes from peppercorns. You can buy pepper already ground into small, even particles. Or, you can buy whole peppercorns and grind your own pepper. Pepper from the grinder is called fresh-ground pepper. It has a fresh, spicy, **delicious** taste!

Get Fresh!

Dried herbs are stronger than fresh herbs. If you substitute fresh herbs for dried herbs, use at least three times as much as the recipe calls for. For example, if the recipe says 1 teaspoon dried basil, use 3 teaspoons chopped fresh basil.

15

Super-Duper Subs

The perfect sandwiches to please a crowd!

MAKES 8 SANDWICHES

TOOLS: Cutting board Rubber spatula Prep bowls Toothpicks
Serrated knife Small sharp knife Plastic wrap

1 Use a **serrated** knife to slice the bread along the long side. Don't cut all the way through to the other side. The bread should open like a book.

2 Spread the mayonnaise along one surface of the bread.

3 Place the slices of cheese along the other surface. Place the meat evenly on top of the cheese.

4 Place layers of vegetables on top of the meat.

5 Close the sandwich carefully and wrap it in plastic wrap. Put it in the refrigerator for at least an hour.

6 Remove the plastic wrap when you are ready to serve the sandwich. Put 8 toothpicks through the sandwich at even intervals. Then slice between the toothpicks with a serrated knife.

Variations

> Choose different sliced meats and cheeses. Altogether, you need 1½ pounds of meat and cheese for each sub. Try pastrami, corned beef, and Swiss cheese. Or try roast beef and Cheddar cheese. Invent your own **delicious** combinations!

> Don't have French bread? Make individual subs in hot-dog buns.

> Drizzle a little bit of Italian dressing on the vegetables.

> Instead of mayonnaise, spread the bread with creamy ranch or Caesar dressing.

Even Cooler!

For a wild and spicy sub, add pepper jack cheese, sliced jalapeño peppers, or horseradish sauce.

Salad in Your Pocket

A salad and a sandwich to go!

MAKES 6 SANDWICHES

INGREDIENTS

Pocket bread (3 6-inch rounds)
6 leaves of leaf lettuce

FOR EGG SALAD

6 eggs, hard-boiled
2 scallions, finely chopped
1 rib celery, finely chopped
⅓ cup mayonnaise
¼ teaspoon salt

FOR TUNA SALAD

2 6-ounce cans tuna
1 egg, hard-boiled
2 scallions, finely chopped
1 rib celery, finely chopped
⅓ cup mayonnaise
¼ teaspoon salt

TOOLS:

Cutting board
Small sharp knife
Measuring spoons

Measuring cups
Prep bowls
Mixing bowls

Can opener
Fork
Saucepan with cover

Timer
Rubber spatula
Strainer

EGG-SALAD POCKETS

1 Cut the eggs in half and then chop them into small pieces.

2 Put the chopped eggs, scallions, and celery in a mixing bowl. Add the mayonnaise and salt. Mix gently with a fork until everything is blended.

3 Cut the 3 pocket bread rounds in half. Gently open each one along the cut edge to form the pocket.

4 Tuck 1 piece of lettuce inside the pocket, then spread ½ cup of the egg salad evenly over the lettuce.

5 Serve the sandwiches immediately, or wrap them in plastic wrap and refrigerate them.

How to Hard-Boil Eggs

1. Put the eggs in a medium saucepan. Cover the eggs with cold water. The water level should be one inch above the eggs.

2. Put the uncovered pan on the stove and turn the burner to medium high. Bring the water to a boil.

3. Reduce the heat to medium. Boil the eggs for 3 minutes.

4. Cover the pan and turn off the heat. Let the eggs sit for 17 minutes.

5. Put the pan in the sink and take the cover off. Get an adult to help with this.

6. Run cold water over the eggs until they are cool.

7. Tap the large end of an egg on the counter to crack it. Remove the shell completely. It's easier to peel an egg if you hold it under running water.

TUNA-SALAD POCKETS

1 Open the cans of tuna with a can opener. Put a strainer in the sink and empty the tuna into it. Rinse the tuna with cold water. Put the tuna in a mixing bowl and fluff it with a fork.

2 Cut the egg in half and chop it into small pieces.

3 Put the chopped egg, scallions, and celery in the mixing bowl with the tuna. Add the mayonnaise and salt. Mix gently with a fork until everything is blended.

4 Assemble the sandwiches as in steps 3 and 4 on the previous page.

5 Serve the sandwiches immediately, or wrap them in plastic wrap and refrigerate them.

TIP: Soften the pocket bread in a toaster oven or a regular oven. Put the bread on a baking sheet in a 350-degree oven for about 3 minutes. Let the bread cool enough to handle before you fill it.

Variations

> Add chopped dill pickle or sunflower seeds to the egg salad or the tuna salad. If you like a creamier sandwich, spread mayonnaise inside the pocket bread before you stuff it.

> Put alfalfa sprouts, avocado slices, or slices of tomato in the pocket bread along with the salad. Use chopped red onion instead of scallions.

Even Cooler!

Add some chopped fresh herbs to either salad. Fresh dill, parsley, and chives are good choices.

Make It a Wrap!

A sandwich that's ready to roll when you are!

It's easy to make a pocket sandwich into a wrap. Just use 6-inch flour tortillas instead of the pocket bread.

1 Put a lettuce leaf over the tortilla.

2 Put ½ cup of the salad mixture (pages 19 - 20) on the lettuce.

3 Fold in one side of the tortilla one inch.

4 Fold the side of the tortilla closest to you over the middle. Be sure the folded edge stays inside.

5 Roll the tortilla over one more time, and you have a wrap!

Make It & Take It

Tips for keeping food you take fresh, delicious, and safe!

Important!

If a recipe contains mayonnaise, eggs, or meat, it needs to be kept cold. If it's not kept cold, it can develop bacteria that can make you sick. Always pack these foods in an **insulated** cooler with ice or **reusable** freezer blocks.

TIP: If you don't have reusable freezer blocks, freeze some juice boxes until they are solid. They will keep your food cold, and the slushy juice is a **delicious** treat!

Plastic wrap is great for wrapping food to take with you. Or, you can use waxed paper.

Aluminum foil is not a good choice. It can cause a reaction with foods that have acid in them. For example, tomatoes will cause the foil to break down.

If you are packing a salad, use a plastic container with a tight-fitting top.

Put plastic-wrapped items into a **resealable** bag. Save the bags to wash and reuse.

A soft-sided **insulated** lunch bag is perfect for taking food anywhere. Pack a school lunch, a picnic, or snacks for a game. Use freezer blocks in this type of bag. Ice cubes will melt and leak through the soft material. Put the blocks on the bottom of the bag.

Pack the items that need to be kept cold on top of the blocks. Trail mix, chips, and other foods that don't need to be kept cold can go in next. Pack these in small **resealable** bags. You can also use containers with tight-fitting lids.

TIP: Cold drinks can help keep foods in the cooler cold too. Just place them around the items that need to be kept cool. Be careful not to squish the sandwiches though!

TIP: Make your own blocks of ice by freezing water in a mold. Milk cartons and plastic containers make great molds. Fill the molds with water and freeze them. Then run warm water over the outside. Your homemade ice blocks will pop right out. The bigger the block, the longer it lasts.

When you bring food for a crowd, use a hard-sided cooler. Since these containers are watertight, you can put bags of ice cubes or blocks of ice in them.

Create-a-Kabob

Fast, fun, and colorful!

MAKES 6 KABOBS

INGREDIENTS

FOR MEAT AND CHEESE KABOBS

½ pound sliced turkey or roast beef

1-pound block Cheddar, Swiss, or mozzarella cheese

FOR VEGGIE AND CHEESE KABOBS

1-pound block Cheddar, Swiss, or mozzarella cheese

24 cherry tomatoes

2 large carrots, peeled and sliced into ½-inch rounds

FOR FRUIT KABOBS

1 melon, such as cantaloupe or honeydew

24 seedless green grapes

24 small strawberries

TOOLS: Cutting board | Spoon | Peeler
Small sharp knife | Melon scoop
Prep bowls | Skewers or toothpicks

1. Cut the meat into 1-inch slices. Make the cuts lengthwise so you have long slices. Roll each slice of meat into a little **cylinder**.

2. Cut the cheese into cubes. First make cuts across the short side. Space your cuts evenly and about ¾ inch apart. Then turn each piece sideways and cut across the cheese to make even pieces.

3. Put the sharp end of a **skewer** through a piece of cheese. Push the cheese part of the way down the skewer.

4. Put a cylinder of meat on the skewer. Poke through the side of the cylinder. Push the meat along the skewer until it touches the cheese.

5. Continue alternating meat and cheese until the skewer is filled.

Even Cooler!

> Make a Hawaiian kabob with ham, chunks of fresh pineapple, and squares of green pepper.

> Make a deli kabob with corned beef, pepper jack cheese, and slices of dill pickle.

Variations

> Add some veggies! Try mushrooms, broccoli, or squares of red or green pepper.

> Make mini kabobs on toothpicks.

VEGGIE AND CHEESE KABOBS

1 Cut the cheese the same way as for the meat and cheese kabobs.

2 Put the ingredients on the **skewer** in a pattern you like. If you start and end with cheese, it will hold the veggies on the skewer.

Even Cooler!

Add large, pitted black olives or chunks of jicama.

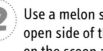

FRUIT KABOBS

1 Cut the melon in half. Scoop out the seeds with a spoon and discard them.

2 Use a melon scoop to make balls of melon. Push the open side of the scoop into the melon. Keep pressure on the scoop and rotate it clockwise.

3 Put the melon ball in a prep bowl. Continue making melon balls until you have used all the melon. Stop scooping before you get to the tough outer skin, or rind, of the melon. It doesn't taste good!

4 Put the ingredients on the skewer in a pattern you like.

Variations

> Use green and red seedless grapes. Try using different kinds of melon. Cantaloupe, honeydew, and gaia are all **delicious** choices! Make mini kabobs on toothpicks with blueberries and raspberries.

INGREDIENTS

Use ½ cup of any four of the following:

Sunflower seeds

Peanuts

Almonds

Pretzel chunks

Sesame sticks

Cashews

Yogurt-dipped raisins

Raisins

Dried cranberries

Dried cherries

Chocolate chips

Coated chocolate candies

IMPORTANT! See note about nut allergies on page 14.

Hit the Trail Mix

MAKES 2 CUPS, ABOUT 4 SERVINGS

A great snack for quick energy and healthy munching!

Put the ingredients in a mixing bowl and stir. The best mixes have some salty and some sweet ingredients. Put ½ cup of the mixture into each of four **resealable** bags. If the trail mix is for a party, just serve it in a bowl instead.

TOOLS: Measuring cups   Spoon
Mixing bowl   Resealable bags

Pasta Salad Presto

It's like having a whole garden in a bowl!

MAKES 8 TO 10 CUPS OF SALAD

INGREDIENTS

FOR THE SALAD

8 ounces bow tie pasta

1 teaspoon salt

2 ounces Parmesan cheese, grated

8 ounces mozzarella cheese, cut in ½-inch cubes

6 radishes, thinly sliced

1 bunch scallions, chopped

2 large carrots, diced

1 small cucumber, peeled, seeded, and diced

1 cup cherry tomatoes

1 green pepper, diced

FOR THE DRESSING

1 clove garlic, finely chopped

¼ cup red wine vinegar

¾ cup olive oil

2 tablespoons fresh parsley, finely chopped

½ teaspoon dried oregano, crumbled

1 teaspoon dried basil, crumbled

½ teaspoon salt

¼ teaspoon pepper

TOOLS:

Cutting board
Small sharp knife
Measuring spoons
Measuring cups

Peeler
Prep bowls
Large mixing bowl
Medium mixing bowl

Whisk
Colander
Wooden spoon
4-quart pot

Timer
Pot holder

PASTA SALAD

1 Fill a 4-quart pot with 3 quarts of cold water. Add 1 teaspoon of salt to the water. Put it on the stove on high heat until the water comes to a rapid boil. This means that the entire surface of the water is moving and bubbling.

2 Add the pasta and stir it briefly with a wooden spoon. Bring the water to a boil again.

3 Turn the heat down to medium high. Set the timer and boil the pasta uncovered. The package will say how long to cook the pasta.

4 Put a colander in the sink. When the timer goes off, ask an adult helper to remove the pan from the heat. Have your helper pour the pasta and cooking water into the colander. Rinse the pasta with cold water. Shake the colander to drain the pasta.

5 Put the drained pasta in a large mixing bowl. Add the Parmesan cheese, the mozzarella cheese, and all the vegetables. Mix well.

6 Make the dressing using the recipe on the next page. Pour the dressing into the bowl. Mix until all the ingredients are **glistening** with the dressing.

7 Cover and refrigerate at least one hour before serving. Stir again before serving.

TIP: Follow these steps to peel and seed a cucumber.

1. Remove the peel with a vegetable peeler.

2. Cut the cucumber in half the long way.

3. Using a spoon held upside down, scrape away the seeds.

ITALIAN DRESSING

1 Put the finely chopped garlic in a medium mixing bowl.

2 Add the red wine vinegar.

3 Pour the olive oil slowly into the vinegar while stirring with a whisk. The vinegar and oil should blend together into a cloudy liquid. If you do not blend them well, they will separate.

4 Add the parsley, oregano, basil, salt, and pepper. Whisk only until these ingredients are mixed in.

Variations

> Use any vegetables or pasta you like! Prepare at least 4 cups of vegetables for 8 ounces of pasta. Try adding broccoli, cauliflower, green beans, zucchini, red onion, avocado, or pitted black or green olives.

> If you don't have a whisk, make the dressing in a jar. Find a jar with a tight-fitting screw top. Put all the ingredients in it and tighten the cap. Shake until the vinegar and oil are blended.

Even Cooler!

> Use fresh herbs instead of dried herbs in the dressing.

> Use balsamic vinegar instead of red wine vinegar.

> Make lemon **vinaigrette** by substituting fresh lemon juice for the vinegar. Add 1 teaspoon of Dijon mustard.

Glossary

cylinder – a solid figure of two parallel circles bound by a curved surface. A soda can is an example of a cylinder.

dangerous – able or likely to cause harm or injury.

delicious – very tasty.

etch – to cut a pattern into a surface with acid or a laser.

glisten – to shine or glitter.

insulate – to keep something from gaining or losing heat by lining it with material.

resealable – able to be opened and closed tightly again and again.

reusable – something that can be used over and over.

serrated – having a jagged edge.

skewer – a long, thin piece of wood or metal used to pierce and hold food.

vinaigrette – a dressing made of oil and vinegar or lemon.

Web Sites

To learn more about cool cooking, visit ABDO Publishing Company on the World Wide Web at **www.abdopublishing.com**. Web sites about cool cooking are featured on our Book Links page. These links are routinely monitored and updated to provide the most current information available.

Index

A

Adult help (for safety), 5, 6, 7, 19. *See also* Safety
Allergies, 14
Aluminum foil, 22

B

Blending, 11

C

Chopping, 11
Cleanliness, 6, 10
Coolers, 9, 22, 23
Cubing, 11

D

Dicing, 11

E

Egg-salad pocket sandwiches, 18, 19

F

Food allergies, 14
Freezer blocks, 22, 23
Fruit kabobs, 24, 26

G

Grating, 10, 11

H

Hard-boiled eggs, 19
Herbs, 15, 20, 30

I

Ice cubes/blocks, 9, 22, 23
Ingredients
    buying, 4
    preparing, 5, 10
    types of, 12–15
Insulated coolers/lunch bags, 9, 22, 23
Italian dressing, 28, 30

K

Kabobs, 24–26
Knives, 6, 7, 8, 10, 11

M

Measuring, 7, 8
Meat and cheese kabobs, 24, 25
Mixing, 11

N

Nut allergies, 14

O

Organic foods, 4

P

Pasta salad, 28–30
Peeling, 10, 29
Pepper, 9, 15
Plastic bags, 9, 22, 23
Plastic containers, 9, 22, 23
Plastic wrap, 9, 22
Pocket sandwiches, 18–20
Preparation (for cooking), 5, 6, 10

R

Resealable bags, 9, 22, 23, 27

S

Safety
    adult help for, 5, 6, 7, 19
    allergies, 14
    guidelines for, 5, 6
    knife use, 6, 7
    storing food, 22–23
    stove and oven use, 5, 6, 7
Salad dressing, 28, 30
Salads, 28–30
Sandwiches, 16–17, 18–20, 21
Slicing, 11
Spices. *See* Herbs; Pepper
Storing food, 22–23
Stove and oven use, 5, 6, 7
Submarine sandwiches, 16–17

T

Terms (for cooking), 4, 10–11
Tools (for cooking), 4, 5, 8–9
Tortillas, 21
Trail mix, 27
Tuna-salad pocket sandwiches, 18, 20

V

Veggie and cheese kabobs, 24, 26

W

Washing (hands, tools, and ingredients), 6, 10
Waxed paper, 9, 22
Weight (of ingredients), 7
Whisking, 11, 30
Wraps, 21